Here to Help

POLICE OFFICER

Rachel Blount

Photography by Bobby Humphrey

W

Franklin Watts
Published in Great Britain in 2017 by The Watts Publishing Group

Credits
Series Editor: Paul Humphrey
Series Designer: D. R. ink
Photographer: Bobby Humphrey
Produced for Franklin Watts by Discovery Books Ltd.

Dewey number: 363.2'2
ISBN: 978 1 4451 3988 3

Printed in China

Franklin Watts
An imprint of
Hachette Children's Group
Part of The Watts Publishing Group
Carmelite House
50 Victoria Embankment
London EC4Y 0DZ

an Hachette UK company
www.hachette.co.uk

www.franklinwatts.co.uk

The publisher and packager would like to thank the following people for their help with this book: West Mercia Police; PC Amanda Watkins and the staff and colleagues at Kidderminster Police Station; Sarah, Richard, Sophie and Jamie Whitehouse; Co-Operative store, Stourport.

Contents

I am a police officer   4

My uniform   6

Meet the team   8

On patrol   10

No seatbelt   12

Foot patrol   14

Emergency call   16

Making an arrest   18

End of shift   20

Helping people   22

When you grow up... & Answers   23

Glossary & Index   24

Words in **bold** are in the glossary on page 24.

I am a police officer

Hello, my name is Amanda and I am a police officer. It is my job to deal with **crime** and keep people safe.

This is my badge.

CONSTABLE WATKINS

?

Can you think of three ways that police officers help us?

This is the police station where I work. Lots of other police officers work here too.

I usually work in the day. Sometimes I work at night. Police officers have to work all through the night so that we can protect people all the time.

There is a big car park where all our vehicles are kept.

My uniform

I wear a police **uniform** when I am at work. This lets people know I am a police officer and that they can come to me if they need help.

I have a radio and an **earpiece**. People who work in the **control room** can talk with me through the radio when I am on **patrol**.

Radio

Earpiece

Hat

Why do police officers wear a hat as part of their uniform?

I also wear a safety vest and a hat.

I wear a belt that holds lots of the **kit** that I may need to do my job.

Safety vest

Belt

PAVA spray

Baton

First aid kit

Handcuffs

Meet the team

At the start of the day I have a meeting with all the other police officers who work in my team. The **sergeant** tells us about any jobs that need to be done.

Where is your nearest police station?

Good morning team. We have a busy day ahead of us.

I have found this purse.

This is Claire. She works behind the front desk at the police station. It is her job to deal with people who come into the station for help or to report a crime.

I check my computer for any emails and then it is time for me to go on patrol.

On patrol

I patrol on my own, unless I am working at night. If I need other police officers to help me I put out a call on my radio. Any police officers that are close by **respond** and then come to help.

Every day is very different when you are a police officer. Some days I visit **victims** of crime, take **statements** from people who have seen a crime, or help people in the street.

Sometimes I use a patrol car. It is white with bright blue and yellow markings. It has lights on the top and a **siren** that makes a loud noise.

When was the last time you saw a police car?

No seatbelt

Today, I see a driver who isn't wearing her seatbelt. Not wearing a seatbelt when you are in a car is a crime and it is also very dangerous. I press a button to put on my patrol car's flashing lights and siren.

?

Why do police officers have flashing lights and sirens on their patrol cars?

The driver pulls over and stops her car. I ask the driver some questions and make some notes in my notepad.

I give the driver a **ticket** because she has committed a crime. I tell her how unsafe she has been. The driver feels very silly and says sorry.

Foot patrol

When I patrol on foot it means I can walk through areas I can't get to in my patrol car. There is an event in town today so PC Max Unitt joins me on patrol.

Are you OK?

At the park I see a little girl who looks upset. Her name is Sophie and she has lost her mum.

I see a woman asking people for help. It is Sophie's mum. Sophie is happy now. I tell her mum how important it is to be careful with children in busy places.

Police officers are friendly people who are there to help you. It is safe to ask them for help.

What should you do if you get lost in a busy place?

There is your mum.

Emergency call

A call comes through on my radio. There has been a theft at one of the shops in town. I need to go and help.

Someone has tried to take something without paying for it. The shop assistant has stopped them from running away.

Can you tell me about the theft?

I take a statement from the shop manager who saw the theft happen.

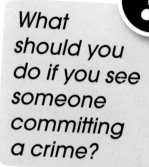

?

What should you do if you see someone committing a crime?

She gives me a receipt for the item the **shoplifter** tried to steal. This is **evidence** that must go back to the station.

Making an arrest

I read the shoplifter a statement. It tells him why he is under **arrest**. Then I put handcuffs on him so that he can't escape and put him in the back of a patrol car.

Back at the station the shoplifter has his fingerprints taken and is put in a **cell**.

Why does a **suspect** have to be placed in a prison cell?

I talk with one of the sergeants and we decide what to do with him. The shoplifter has been filmed on the shop's camera. This means we have enough evidence to **charge** him with shoplifting.

End of shift

It has been a busy day today.

I still have to write up all my notes before I go home. This is an important part of my job. I fill in **reports** for all of the **incidents** I have been to today.

?

Why do you think police officers have to record everything carefully?

I check my notes with PC Unitt. We will hand them over to the team of police officers that are working tonight. They need to know what has happened on my team's shift so that they can take over.

Helping people

I really enjoy being a police officer. There are lots of other staff and police officers who help me to do my job.

Most of all I enjoy helping people, protecting them and making the area where they live a safer place.

I really enjoy my job!

When you grow up...

If you would like to be a police officer or police community support officer here are some simple tips and advice.

What kind of person are you?

- You are friendly and enjoy talking to people
- You enjoy working as part of a team
- You are fit and active
- You are interested in law/crime
- Most of all, you enjoy helping people.

How do you become a police officer?

You can attend a Public Services Course at college or complete a diploma in policing at university.

You can also get involved with the police cadets. For more information see:
www.nationalvpc.org

Answers

P4. Police officers help to prevent crimes by: patrolling our streets; helping us when we report a crime; making sure drivers are safe on the roads.

P7. Police officers wear a police hat to protect their head and so that people can see them doing their job and approach them if they need help.

P12. The flashing lights and sirens alert drivers to stop their vehicles or move out of the way.

P15. Find an adult with children, a police officer, or a police community support officer and ask them for help.

P17. Tell an adult who will decide whether they should call the police.

P19. Suspects are placed in cells to keep them safe and secure. It also gives the police officer time to get information together and decide whether or not to charge the suspect.

P20. Police officers record all the details of a crime carefully, this can lead to **criminals** being **convicted**.

Were your answers the same as the ones in this book? Don't worry if they were different, sometimes there is more than one right answer. Talk about your answer with other people. Can you explain why you think your answer is right?

Glossary

arrest to take someone to the police station when it is thought they have committed a crime

baton a short, heavy stick that is used by police officers to protect themselves

cell a small room in a police station where someone who has been arrested is held

charge to lawfully accuse someone of committing a crime

control room a control centre where people answer emergency calls from the public. They then send police officers to attend.

convicted to be found guilty of committing a crime

crime something that is wrong or against the law

criminals people who have committed crimes

earpiece a small piece of plastic that fits into the ear and is connected to an officer's radio

evidence items, belongings, or statements that are connected to a crime

handcuffs a pair of linked metal rings that lock together to secure someone's hands together

incidents events

kit equipment that police officers might need to do their job

patrol to keep watch over an area

PAVA spray a chemical spray used by the police if they need to protect themselves

reports written statements of an event

respond answer

sergeant a police officer who is in charge of other police officers

shoplifter someone who has tried to take something from a shop without paying for it

siren a loud warning sound

statements written recordings of an event

suspect a person who is suspected of committing a crime

ticket a piece of paper given to someone who has committed a driving crime

uniform special clothing worn by people who belong to the same organisation

victims people who have been affected by crime

Index

arrest 18-19

control room 6

crime 4, 9, 10, 12-13, 16-19, 23

criminals 12-13, 17-19, 23

emergency call 16-17

equipment 6-7, 10, 16, 18

evidence 17, 19

patrol 6, 9, 10-11, 12, 14-15, 23

police officers 4-5, 6-7, 8, 10, 12, 15, 20, 21, 23

police station 5, 8, 9, 17, 19

police vehicles 5, 11, 12, 18, 23

sergeant 8, 19

siren 11, 12, 23

uniform 6-7

victim 10